This Book Belongs To:

Made in the USA
Coppell, TX
20 November 2019

11665765R00069